Drawing Near

Praise for *Drawing Near*

If there were ever a book of devotions for the nature lover, Pasquale Mingarelli's *Drawing Near: A Devotional Meeting God in His Creation* is the one that should be on every bookshelf … or backpack. Mingarelli beautifully combines his love for nature photography with his love for the Lord in a powerful book that will draw you closer to God while simultaneously allowing you to appreciate the glory and splendor of His creation.

—**John Farrell**, Digital Content Manager, Inspiration Ministries

Drawing Near is a work that is destined to linger in the lives of those who experience its message. The photography that sets the table for each daily devotion is on par with the best ever taken in nature. They captivate the eyes; the words touch the soul, and the Scripture references cleanse all aspects of our daily lives. Pasquale Mingarelli has brought a devotional that is easy to read, biblically accurate, and destined to be a treasure for decades to come.

—**Pete Rogers**, host of *Christian Outdoors Podcast* and author of *Do You Enjoy God? 12 Steps to Enjoying God Everyday*

As a Christian wilderness camp director, I spend countless hours in the outdoors drawing near to God. I find peace there. In *Drawing Near*, Pasquale captures the peace of God and the connection to Him that creation offers us. He writes like someone who has met God while spending time in the outdoors. In *Drawing Near*, Pasquale brings that connection to you so that you can experience God in the outdoors whether you can make it outside yourself or not.

—**Daniel Wahlgren**, Camp Director, Table in the Wilderness Camp, Centennial, Wyoming

I have long been a follower of Pasquale Mingarelli's daily posts the "Visual Verse of the Day." They are always uplifting, include relevant Scripture verses, and are accompanied by beautiful nature, wildlife, or other outdoor photographs that visually reinforce both the Bible verse he quotes and his comments. They have long been a part of my daily devotionals, so I was especially pleased to learn that he is publishing a daily devotional book titled, *Drawing Near: Meeting God in His Creation*.

I am delighted to endorse this timely, unique, wonderful daily devotional.

—**Dan Story**, MA, author of dozens of nature articles and eight books including, *Should Christians Be Environmentalists?* and *Will Dogs Chase Cats in Heaven?*

On day five of reading *Drawing Near*, I found myself at the Norris Peak lookout station in the majestic Black Hills of South Dakota. As I looked at the pictures, the words from the page somehow became more vivid. "From Everlasting to Everlasting" suddenly spoke powerfully to me. And while I read "The Eagle Soars," I literally looked up in the brilliant blue sky and watched an eagle gracefully rise up from the bottom of this valley into full flight above me.

If I could encourage you to gaze through Pasquale's photographs and walk with him through the Scriptures, I certainly would. Additionally, I might suggest somewhere early in your reading that you find a secluded spot, if not a mountain, and allow the pages of God's Word and the beauty of this work to assist you in drawing near.

—**Rusty Miller**, pastor, Bellevue, Nebraska

PASQUALE MINGARELLI

MEETING GOD *in*
HIS CREATION

DRAWING
Near

A DEVOTIONAL

NASHVILLE

NEW YORK • LONDON • MELBOURNE • VANCOUVER

Drawing Near

Meeting God in His Creation

Published in New York, New York, by Morgan James Publishing. Morgan James is a trademark of Morgan James, LLC. www.MorganJamesPublishing.com

Proudly distributed by Ingram Publisher Services.

Unless otherwise indicated, Scripture quotations are taken from the New American Standard Bible 1995® (NASB 1995), Copyright © 1960, 1962, 1963, 1968, 1971, 1972, 1973, 1975, 1977, 1995 by The Lockman Foundation. Used by permission. www.Lockman.org.

Scripture quotations marked (NIV) are taken from the Holy Bible, New International Version®, NIV®. Copyright © 1973, 1978, 1984, 2011 by Biblica, Inc.™ Used by permission of Zondervan. All rights reserved worldwide. www.zondervan.comThe "NIV" and "New International Version" are trademarks registered in the United States Patent and Trademark Office by Biblica, Inc.™

Scripture quotations marked (NKJV) are taken from the New King James Version®. Copyright © 1982 by Thomas Nelson. Used by permission. All rights reserved.

Morgan James BOGO™

A **FREE** ebook edition is available for you or a friend with the purchase of this print book.

CLEARLY SIGN YOUR NAME ABOVE

Instructions to claim your free ebook edition:
1. Visit MorganJamesBOGO.com
2. Sign your name CLEARLY in the space above
3. Complete the form and submit a photo of this entire page
4. You or your friend can download the ebook to your preferred device

ISBN 9781636980584 paperback
ISBN 9781636980591 ebook
Library of Congress Control Number: 2022945825

Cover & Interior Design by:
Christopher Kirk
www.GFSstudio.com

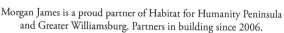

Morgan James PUBLISHING Builds with... Habitat for Humanity Peninsula and Greater Williamsburg

Morgan James is a proud partner of Habitat for Humanity Peninsula and Greater Williamsburg. Partners in building since 2006.

Get involved today! Visit: www.morgan-james-publishing.com/giving-back

Table of Contents

DRAWING *Near*

Introduction

Mills Lake Trail, Rocky Mountain National Park, Colorado

M any heroes in the Bible spent time connecting with God in the wilderness. Even Jesus headed to the wilderness. Over a dozen times, the Gospels mention Jesus going alone into nature or to a quiet place to meet with the Father. The Gospel of Luke says He did it often (Luke 5:16).

Today, we miss that. Fewer and fewer people head out to nature to spend time with our Heavenly Father. Those of us who do, know that nature is a great place to connect with Him. God reveals Himself through His creation. Creation speaks to us about God, and God speaks to us through His creation.

I wrote this devotional because so much in our world today keeps people from drawing near to God. We often find it hard to get outside and seek the Lord there. I desire to help people meet God and see Him in the natural world. I want to help them draw near to Him. Like the heroes in the Bible, when we spend time with God in the outdoors, we do draw near.

Take this devotional with you when you get outside. Reading it outdoors is a wonderful way to enjoy it and fully experience it! But if you cannot get outdoors, use this devotional to help you better understand what nature and being outside can tell us about God. Either way, may it help you draw near to God and connect with Him.

Nature reveals God to us. The Bible mentions nature, or the wilderness, and it does so to reveal different attributes about its Creator. The Bible uses creation:

- To reveal God's glory, splendor, and majesty
- To speak of His greatness, power, and other characteristics
- As metaphors to describe what our Lord is like

- To explain how He is our refuge and our salvation
- As illustrations to show how God provides for us
- To tell us how great of a Creator our God is

For this devotional, I compiled forty verses or passages of Scripture that use nature in some way to point us to God. These forty verses and passages do not come from the creation account in Genesis. I wanted people to see that the Bible says a lot about nature beyond the creation story in Genesis.

Even though I eliminated the Genesis account, I found the work of scaling down the hundreds of creation references outside of Genesis to forty a bit challenging but insightful.

The verses and passages in this devotional are divided into four topics. Each devotion will have an icon next to it representing the topic it belongs to. The four topics and icons are as follows:

God's Greatness, Power, and Other Revealed Attributes

Praise and Worship to Our Glorious Majestic God

Our Protector, Refuge, Deliverer, and Salvation

Our Great Creator and Provider

I asked the readers of my online devotional, the Visual Bible Verse of the Day, what they desired to see in a devotional book. They wanted the devotions to dig into God's Word, to be personal, and to contain a prayer. In response to my readers' requests, each entry will contain four short sections, plus a prayer: "In the Word," "In Context," In "Nature," "In Us," and "In Prayer."

I pray you draw near to God as you read through this devotional and dwell on His Word. May He speak to your heart.

Knowing God: A Note for Those Who Are Not Familiar with Jesus

Saint Louis River, Jay Cooke State Park, Minnesota

A s a young photographer, I subscribed to two magazines to help me improve my skills. One was *Outdoor Photographer,* and the other was *National Geographic.* I found both magazines to be helpful and inspiring. *Outdoor Photographer* did that from the insight and tips in its articles and from the photographs that glossed its pages. *National Geographic* did so through its use of outstanding photography. Although I enjoyed *Geographic's* (what we photographers called it) articles, often I found myself methodically flipping through, looking at the photographs.

One article I remember reading back in the day was about Alaska. *Geographic* often uses the stories of several different individuals to tell the story of a place. And this particular article told the story of one of Alaska's many nature lovers. The man spoke of how he loved spending time in the outdoors and experiencing the spirituality he found in nature. The man could not specifically articulate what the spiritual experience or presence was that he found in nature, but he knew it was there.

I, too, find something spiritual in the beauty, peace, and wonder of nature. Many others do as well but just can't place their finger on what that spiritual presence is. Some think of it as the spirit of the woods, the mountain, the lake, the river, or something else.

The famous Dutch artist, Vincent van Gogh, who was not known for his faith, also felt something spiritual in nature, only he found it to be of God. He wrote, "When I have a terrible need of—shall I say the word—religion, then I go out and paint the stars."[1]

---

1   Vincent Van Gogh, letters of Vincent van Gogh, September 28, 1888

The apostle Paul also wrote about how God is revealed in nature. In the Bible's book of Romans (chapters 1 and 10), he explained why we find a spiritual presence in nature. He tells us that nature reveals God. I agree with Paul and van Gogh. Nature proclaims that God exists. Nature tells us He is beautiful, wonderful, loving, redemptive, perfect peace, and so much more.

If you find, peace, beauty, and wonder in nature and feel that spiritual presence there but just can't figure it out, I recommend that you seek out the answer in the Bible and in Jesus. The beauty, peace, and wonder we find in nature, point to Jesus. In Him alone, we will find ultimate peace, beauty, and wonder. Sadly, if we decide not to follow Jesus, we will never truly discover these things we are longing to find.

I hope as you read this devotional that it will help you on your journey. I also hope you will come to understand that God reveals Himself through His creation and that spiritual presence you feel is nature calling out His name. In nature, we see God's hand and it speaks to our spirit about God.

If you don't know God, I pray you come to know Him. If you want to know Him, confess Jesus as Lord, surrender your life to Him, and turn away from following your own ways to follow His ways. Place your faith and trust in Him. After that, seek out a good church with a community of believers and be baptized there. If you need help finding a good church, email me at pat@thecreationspeaks.com.

Day 1

God's Greatness
and Power

Moon, mountains, meadow and pines,
San Isabel National Forest, Colorado

In the Word

*"Yours, O L*ORD*, is the greatness and the power and the glory and the victory and the majesty, indeed everything that is in the heavens and the earth; Yours is the dominion, O L*ORD*, and You exalt Yourself as head over all."* (1 Chronicles 29:11)

In Context

King David longed to build a temple for God, but God told Him no (1 Chronicles 17) because David had "shed much blood" and "waged great wars" (1 Chronicles 22). The Lord told David He would have a son, Solomon, and Solomon would build the temple because he "shall be a man of rest" (1 Chronicles 22). David didn't sour over the fact that he would not build the temple, but he rejoiced in God's better plan.

In 1 Chronicles 29, David provided material for Solomon to build the temple and offered up a prayer of praise to God for His greatness, power, glory, and victory, as well as proclaiming that God has dominion over "everything that is in the heavens and the earth." By His power, God rules over nature.

In Nature

We see many powerful and amazing things in nature. Think of a mountain or the ocean. They have real *wow* power. But God is far greater than the mountains or the oceans. He is the head over them and all that lives within them.

In Us

David worshipped God for His greatness and power. Knowing that God rules over and controls nature brings thoughts of praise to those who love Him. May we humble ourselves and worship the great God of creation that we serve.

In Prayer

Dear God, I praise You! You reign with dominion over all creation. It exists by You and for You and for us. I glorify Your name. For You are great!

Notes

_____

_____

_____

_____

_____

_____

_____

_____

Day 2

LORD Most High

Bullhead Lake, Glacier National Park, Montana

In the Word

For You are the L<small>ORD</small> *Most High over all the earth; You are exalted far above all gods.* (Psalm 97:9)

In Context

During biblical times, each nation made up its own gods. There were the gods of the Philistines, the gods of Egyptians, the gods of the Canaanites, and so on. But these man-made gods were only the gods of one nation or people. Those gods disappeared with the ancient people who worshipped them. By contrast, Yahweh, the God of Israel, claimed to be the everlasting God above all other gods and that all nations would someday worship Him.

In Nature

In my younger days, I use to say, "I never saw a rock I didn't want to be on top of." I enjoyed standing on top of a mountain, hill, or rock. I loved the view and having things below me. But no matter how high I got, there was always something higher—another land formation, a bird, the clouds, the sky. Yet God is the most high above all the earth and everything else. He looks down on all creation. Even the stars.

In Us

Just as the mountains tower above the landscape below, God's greatness rises far above any fictitious deity created by mortal men. His greatness rises higher than anything we may put before Him. When we give more time and treasure to something on earth than we do to God, it serves only our own useless vanity.

We are far better off making God first and all other things second. As the Lord Most High, God desires to rank first above all else.

In Prayer

O Lord Most High above all the earth, help me to keep You first in my life. Keep me from vain idols. I want to worship You as the one true God.

Notes

_____

_____

_____

_____

_____

_____

_____

Day 3

Made White as Snow

Snow and hoarfrost on farmland, Sarpy County, Nebraska

In the Word

"Come now, and let us reason together," says the LORD, *"Though your sins are as scarlet, they will be as white as snow; though they are red like crimson, they will be like wool."* (Isaiah 1:18)

In Context

In Isaiah chapters 1 to 39, the prophet wrote about God's coming destruction of the ancient people of Judea. He wrote a long list of sins and God's consequences upon those sins. In the middle of all the condemnation, Isaiah said all the people needed to do was turn from their sins and God would make them clean (Isaiah 1:18–19).

Sin is refuse before God, yet He promised the people He would wipe their sin clean if they repented and followed Him. Sadly, they did not, and judgment fell upon their nation.

In Nature

As the sun rose one February morning, a hoarfrost made the newly fallen snow shine. I knew I had to go out and photograph the landscape. I put my two preschoolers in the car and off we went.

I drove down many country roads that morning and captured some beautiful images (like the one illustrating this devotion). To this day, the images speak to me about the purity of God. He makes the snow pure, and He alone washes away our sins, making us as perfectly pure as the snow.

In Us

Romans 3:23 tells us we all have sinned. Each one of us stands defiled before God, deserving His wrath and judgment. But while we were yet sinners, God sent His son Jesus to die for the forgiveness of our sins. Through Jesus, we can be made white as snow. If you have never repented of your sin and turned to Jesus, you can do so at this very moment. See "In Prayer" below.

In Prayer

Jesus, I repent of my sin against You and turn to You for salvation and eternal life. Thank You for dying on the cross for me. I accept Your free gift of salvation and have decided to follow You as Savior and Lord of my life. Amen.

Notes

_____

_____

_____

_____

_____

_____

_____

Day 4

Feeding Those Who Need to Be Fed

Tree sparrows, Bellevue, Nebraska

In the Word

They all wait for You to give them their food in due season. You give to them, they gather it up; You open Your hand, they are satisfied with good. (Psalm 104:27–28)

In Context

Psalm 104 celebrates God as Creator and Caretaker of His creation. It shows how God, in His wisdom, not only created but He created in a way in which things of creation are interconnected.

The psalm also points out that God remains active and personal in creation today. He provides for and cares for His creatures until death (verses 29–30). The food they eat comes from God Who kindly gives it to them.

In Nature

Nature feeds nature. It's wonderful to watch it work. All we need to do is to observe a wild field. The grasses and flowers grow. The butterflies and bees sip sweet nectar and spread pollen to grow more flowers. The rabbits and ground squirrels hide in the grasses, fertilizing the ground with their droppings. And when they stray from cover, a hawk swoops down and God provides for the hawk. Nature works because God makes it work.

In Us

God provides for His creatures, but sometimes, He uses us to do it. We set up a couple of birdfeeders in our yard. When the birds come to eat, I think about Psalm 104 and how God is using us to provide for His creatures. God doesn't need us to feed His creatures, but He chooses to use us. And God doesn't need us to spread His Word, but He chooses to use us. It's an honor to feed His creation, but it's a greater honor to feed a soul who needs to hear about Jesus.

In Prayer

God, it's fun to feed Your creatures but also help me feed those who need to hear about You. Give me a heart that's ready to serve.

Notes

Day 5

Everlasting to Everlasting

Mount Moran from Colter Bay, Grand Teton National Park, Wyoming

In the Word

Before the mountains were born or You gave birth to the earth and the world, even from everlasting to everlasting, You are God. (Psalm 90:2)

In Context

Moses wrote Psalm 90. The whole psalm speaks of the greatness of God. It compares the greatness of God to human mortality.

Verse 2 tells us how great God is by saying He has always been God. The old-time Bible teacher Dr. J. Vernon McGee says *from everlasting to everlasting* means "from vanishing point to vanishing point" In other words, God existed before time and will still exist when time disappears. He is eternal.

God created time and exists outside of it. Time does not and cannot hold God. Farther down in Psalm 90, verse 4 says, *For a thousand years in Your sight are like yesterday when it passes by, or as a watch in the night.* With God, the day-to-day has little significance.

In Nature

When Moses wrote this psalm, he and the Hebrew people were wandering in the desert where Moses would've seen mountains. In my hikes in the desert, the mountains appear exceptionally durable. Without tress to cover them, they look like indestructible giant rocks. Without soil over them, one can feel how solid they are. Moses observed these qualities of the desert mountains when he wrote, *Before the mountains were born . . . You are God.* Even though the mountains looked like they had been around forever, Moses pointed out that God existed long before them.

In Us

Passing time is nothing to God. While we build our life around time and cannot get enough, it is minuscule to God. He controls it. It does not control Him. When I struggle with my inefficiencies, I lose sight of the fact that God is the father of time. He never worries about how much I am not getting done. When I look to God with a clear mind, I find encouragement in knowing that He controls time.

In Prayer

Dear God, help me to know that You hold time in Your hands. When I feel the rush of the world and don't get done what I think I need to get done, help me to find Your peace.

Notes

_____

_____

_____

_____

_____

_____

_____

Day 6

Sing for Joy

Inlet, Acadia National Park, Maine

In the Word

Let the heavens be glad, and let the earth rejoice; Let the sea roar, and all it contains; Let the field exult, and all that is in it. Then all the trees of the forest will sing for joy. (Psalm 96:11–12)

In Context

Psalm 96 is a celebratory psalm of praise that is known as a royal psalm. In each of its first three lines, the psalm uses the word *sing*. The Scripture often repeats words or phrases three times. It does so to emphasize and show significance. The use of the word *sing* three times at the beginning of this psalm sets the attitude for the entire psalm. It applauds the greatness of God with great celebration! And it calls people and all creation to sing.

In Nature

On cool spring mornings, I like to sit out on our deck to spend time with God. On these mornings, nature sings. The birds chirp, rambunctious squirrels forage, bunnies bounce, green covers the ground, and leaves begin to emerge on awakening branches, covering once naked trees. As I sit and pray, I sense that all creation is singing and celebrating God. My heart takes pleasure in creation's song.

In Us

Psalm 96 calls us to celebrate the greatness of God. When we look at creation, we certainly can see that God is great. He designed it that way so we would worship Him there and take pleasure in His creation.

May the greatness of God revealed in His creation bring a song to our hearts. When you hear creation sing, join in and sing for joy at the greatness of God. He is a good God.

In Prayer

Dear God, when I look at the wonders of creation and listen to it sing to You, I want to sing to You as well. May creation remind me of how great You are.

Notes

Day 7

Firmly Planted

Stone Creek in Platte River State Park, Nebraska

In the Word
How blessed is the man who does not walk in the counsel of the wicked, nor stand in the path of sinners, nor sit in the seat of scoffers . . . He will be like a tree firmly planted by streams of water, which yields its fruit in its season and its leaf does not wither; and in whatever he does, he prospers. (Psalm 1:1–3)

In Context
What a wonderful way to start the book of Psalms with such a great promise! *The Ryrie Study Bible* says Psalm 1 "stands as a faithful door keeper" for the whole book of Psalms. The psalm reminds us that righteous behavior and the fruitful life are characteristics of those who delight in God's law.

In Nature
Psalm 1 gives us a wonderful picture from nature of what the life of a faithful believer looks like. Trees thrive near water, and they grow tall. Without much water, they struggle to grow or do not grow at all. But when they prosper, trees bless those around them with fruit, shade, and other good things. The tree's prosperity is for others and not just the tree.

Before European settlers moved onto the Great Plains in North America, trees were sparse. One place the cottonwoods and other trees stood tall was by rivers where water provided them with life and protection from fire. Out on the open prairie, without water, trees failed to grow or burned in prairie fires.

In Us

If we want to grow in our faith, we need to read God's Word and delight in it. To delight in God's Word means we find enjoyment by reading it and living by it. When we do these things, the Scripture assures us that we will prosper. When we spiritually prosper, we grow in our faith and bless others. Like trees, our prosperity is more about others than it is about us.

In Prayer

Dear Lord, help me to delight in You and Your Word more and more each day. Work in me that I may grow, and work through me that I may touch others.

Notes

Day 8

True Independence

Longs Peak and Moraine Park, Rocky Mountain National Park, Colorado

In the Word

"In the beginning, Lord, you laid the foundations of the earth, and the heavens are the work of your hands. They will perish, but you remain; they will all wear out like a garment. You will roll them up like a robe; like a garment they will be changed." (Hebrews 1:10–12 NIV)

In Context

Hebrews 1 brings up several important theological concepts. Let's look at two of them. One is the deity of Jesus Christ. Verse 8 says, "But of the Son He says, 'YOUR THRONE, OH GOD, IS FOREVER AND EVER.'" The context of verse 8 makes it clear that the "He" is God the Father, and He calls His son, Jesus, "God."

Hebrews 1:10–12 also reveals that, in the beginning, God created everything and that He is not part of creation. God exists independent of creation. God does not need the help of creation to exist. Everything in creation needs the help of creation and the help of God to exist. God alone is self-existent.

In Nature

Everything in nature relies on other things in nature. Every tree we see needs the sun and the dirt. All animals need food. All fish need water. And every mammal needs air. Even parasites need a host. Everything is part of what some would call, "the circle of life."

Psalm 104 shows (see Day 4) how nature depends on nature and how nature depends on God. God alone depends on nothing.

In Us

God not needing any help from anything or anyone means, "He's got this." Nothing happens in our lives that He can't control. God is great. He not only holds the entire universe but our trials and troubles as well.

In Prayer

God, I praise You that You created everything and are great beyond my imagination! Thank You for being in control.

Notes

_____

_____

_____

_____

_____

_____

_____

Day 9

The Eagle Soars . . .
And I Don't
Know Why?

Bald eagle, Lake Manawa State Park, Iowa

In the Word

"Does the eagle soar at your command and build its nest on high? It dwells on a cliff and stays there at night; a rocky crag is its stronghold." (Job 39:27–28 NIV)

In Context

In Job 39, God shows Job how wise and wonderful He is. The Lord lists many wild animals and asks Job if he (Job) created them and gave them their powers or if he controls the things of nature? And Job could only listen in humble speechlessness.

God used the animals to show Job he could in no way question God. He used nature to show Job how much he did not know about God's ways. God created everything and possesses infinite wisdom and power. He answers to no one, and He knows what He is doing.

In Nature

My wife loves bald eagles. She knows how to appreciate these magnificent birds God created. While I am busy photographing them, she sits and enjoys them. She watches them soar with ease and admires how regal they look in the sky, perched high in a nest, or even on the ground. The sight of these birds inspires my wife and many others. Our infinite God, in His creativity, imagined them, engineered them, and commands each one of them.

In Us

God knew what He was doing when He created eagles. He always knows what He is doing. We often don't understand why things happen, but God does. Like Job, we often question God, but He is the one who designed nature and designed us. He calls us to trust Him and tells us, as He told Job, that we do not know all that He knows. The maker and keeper of the eagles is worthy of our trust.

In Prayer

Dear Lord, help me to trust You, even though I don't understand. Help me rest in knowing that I may never understand why life is as it is.

Notes

_____

_____

_____

_____

_____

_____

_____

Day 10

Delight and Study

Cow elk grazing, Rocky Mountain National Park, Colorado

In the Word

Great are the works of the Lord; They are studied by all who delight in them. Splendid and majestic is His work, and His righteousness endures forever. (Psalm 111:2–3)

In Context

The works of creation, great or small, point to their Creator. Psalm 111 is an act of praise, rejoicing in God's creation as it worships Him. In praise and gratitude, it celebrates God's compassion, covenant, wisdom, and provision for those who fear Him.

In Nature

While hiking down a mountain in Colorado with one of my nephews, he spotted an elk grazing in the woods. I pulled out my camera, took a few steps off the trail, and began to photograph her. As I clicked, she glanced at me with cautious brown eyes but continued eating. Both my nephew and I marveled at her beauty and gentle majesty. We saw the wonder of the Creator in her and took delight in His creation.

In Us

People who delight in nature, study nature. People who delight in God, study God. People who delight in nature and in God, study the creation and see the many ways it points to God, and they rejoice!

Find a simple thing in nature, such as an acorn, a flower, an ant, a piece of fruit, or even a small stream. Take delight in it and ask the question, "What does this tell me about God?" Write down your thoughts. You'll be amazed by what such simple things can teach us about God.

In Prayer
Dear Lord, help me to delight in You and Your Word more and more each day. Work in me that I may grow, and work through me that I may touch others.

Notes

_____

_____

_____

_____

_____

_____

_____

Day 11

The Protection
of His Wings

Great egret nesting, Central Florida

In the Word

He will cover you with his feathers, and under his wings you will find refuge; his faithfulness will be your shield and rampart. (Psalm 91:4 NIV)

In Context

Psalm 91 praises God for His protection. In addition to verse 4, some other familiar passages come from this psalm, such as verse 1, which states, *He who dwells in the shelter of the Most High will abide in the shadow of the Almighty.* And verse 11, *For He will give His angels charge concerning you, to guard you in all your ways.*

Psalm 91 proclaims that God's protection is there for us under the stipulation that we need to make Him our dwelling place (verses 1 and 11). If we don't stay close to God, we have no promise of His protection.

In Nature

Did you ever see one of those videos in which a goose chases somebody? Or have you ever witnessed someone being divebombed by an angry bird, and I am not talking about the video game? Birds, both great and small, are dedicated, protective parents.

Birds in the nest make for extra protective parents. They cover their chicks to hide them from potential predators and to shelter them from the elements. The writer of Psalm 91 draws on the protective character traits of birds to illustrate God's protection of us.

In Us

God covers us, shelters us, and draws us close, but we need to stay in His nest. Staying in God's nest doesn't mean we hide from the world in churches and in fellowship. God calls us to be out in the world doing His work and living our lives. But staying in God's nest means to spiritually dwell with Him. It means to be in the world but not of the world.

To stay in God's nest, He says we need to read His Word and live the way He desires us to live. He calls us to serve Him and others and live according to His standards.

In Prayer
Lord, thank You for Your loving protection and shelter. Help me to stay close to You.

Notes

_____

_____

_____

_____

_____

_____

_____

Day 12

General Revelation

Sunset sky, Loess Bluffs National Wildlife Refuge, Missouri

In the Word

The heavens are telling of the glory of God; and their expanse is declaring the work of His hands. Day to day pours forth speech, and night to night reveals knowledge . . . Their line has gone out through all the earth, and their utterances to the end of the world. (Psalm 19:1–2, 4a)

In Context

Through His wisdom, God created the universe. He left His fingerprints in creation so that it all points to Him. Psalm 19 says creation tells us of the glory of God. Theologians call this "general revelation."

General revelation is just that, general. It's not specific nor spelled out in writing, and it's available to everyone.

In Nature

When I lived in Orlando, Florida, my parents would often visit. During their visits, we stayed at the beach. I loved getting up early to photograph the sunrise, the ocean, and the critters of the beach. In the quiet roar of the surf, the warming sun, and endless ocean horizon, I felt the presence of God. Through the subtle power of general revelation, nature spoke to me of the wonder of God.

In Us

Nature speaks to our hearts about God. No one who looks, listens, and studies nature can truly deny the existence of a god. But nature does not give us specific details of who God is. That is why He has given us the Bible. In the Bible alone, we learn about Jesus, the depths of God's love, and all that He has done for us. In the Bible alone, we find out who God truly is. That is why He calls us to study it. The more we study it, the more we learn about Him.

In Prayer
Dear God, help me to find You in nature, but more importantly, help me to dive deep into the Bible so I truly know You.

Notes

_____

_____

_____

_____

_____

_____

_____

_____

Day 13

God Preserves Man
and Animal

Mountain goats, Glacier National Park, Montana

In the Word

Your righteousness is like the mountains of God; Your judgments are like a great deep. O LORD, You preserve man and beast. (Psalm 36:6)

In Context

Psalm 36 contrasts the goodness of God with the sinfulness of humanity. It begins by condemning the wicked in verses 1–4. In verse 5, it transitions into praising God and mentions His loving devotion and faithfulness. In verses 5–6, it uses two images from nature to proclaim great and wonderful things about God: His faithfulness and righteousness. Verses 7–11 mention that God blesses and takes care of humankind.

In Nature

The psalm uses the sky and the clouds to show us how far-reaching God's faithfulness is. When you look up at the sky and see how far away it all seems, know that God's faithfulness extends just as far and even farther.

Verse 6 compares God's righteousness to mountains to explain that God's righteousness is great. Do we see anything on earth that is greater than a mountain? If we stand in a mountain town or valley and look around, we see nothing that compares to the greatness of the mountains. Psalm 36 tells us nothing compares to the righteousness of God.

In Us

Righteousness and faithfulness are two of God's attributes. We behold mountains with awe, but we are to live in awe of God's righteousness. God's faithfulness goes without end, like the sky seems to go without end. God always acts in righteousness and faithfulness. We can take comfort in knowing that in His righteousness and faithfulness, He takes care of His creatures, and He takes care of you and me all the more.

In Prayer

Dear Lord, help me to know that Your righteousness is great. May the sky be a reminder to me of how far-reaching your faithfulness is. Thank You for caring for me and all Your creation.

Notes

Day 14

The Heavens Praise God

Sunrise, Fontenelle Forest, Nebraska

In the Word

The heavens will praise Your wonders, O Lord; Your faithfulness also in the assembly of the holy ones. For who in the skies is comparable to the Lord? Who among the sons of the mighty is like the Lord? (Psalm 89:5–6)

In Context

Psalm 89 begins as a song of praise. The first few verses sing of God's mercy and faithfulness. Verse 2 declares that in the heavens, God's faithfulness shall be established. And verse 5 announces that the heavens praise God for His wonders. God's mercy and faithfulness are just two of His many wonders.

Then verse 6 ask the question, *For who in the skies is comparable to the* LORD? The answer is no one. Nothing compares to God. Nothing shines brighter or is more glorious than Him.

In Nature

The beauty and glory in the sky praise God and call us to praise Him. When we look at the sky, we know there is something greater than us, and we know there is something greater than the sky. As glorious as that sunrise or evening sky is, it cannot compare to God. Nothing in nature (and certainly nothing manmade) shines brighter than the glory of God.

In Us

The majesty of the sky's glorious splendor reminds us that God's splendor is revealed both in the heavens and on earth. When we are touched by nature's beauty, may we remember to give praise to our God the Creator, just as the sky praises Him.

In Prayer

Praise You, God, who created all the heavens. I praise You as the heavens do. May my life shine gloriously for You.

Notes

_____

_____

_____

_____

_____

_____

_____

Day 15

He Leads Me Beside Quiet Waters

East Inlet Creek, Rocky Mountain National Park, Colorado

In the Word

The Lord is my shepherd, I shall not want. He makes me lie down in green pastures; He leads me beside quiet waters. He restores my soul; He guides me in the paths of righteousness for His name's sake. (Psalm 23:1–3)

In Context

The *Nelson Study Bible* says that in the ancient Middle East, kings were considered the shepherds of their people. With God as His shepherd or king, the psalmist David knew he could rest and trust in Him. David's shepherd drew him to green pastures by still waters—pastures where he could find peaceful rest and provision. Green pastures not only provide sheep with rest but food as well.

When we look at the subject and verbs in this passage, we see that the shepherd does all the work. *He makes. He leads. He restores. He guides.* God, our shepherd king, takes all the actions. We are to rest in Him.

In Nature

So much about landscape photography is about peace and tranquility. Why? Because when we go to such places, our soul finds rest. Even if it's along the side of the road. When we stop the car, pull over, and wonder, nature still gives us a feeling of peace. Often when I visit such places of peace, I want to stay for a long time. I want to read from the Bible and think about the goodness of God.

In Us

A landscape photo of a lush green pasture can remind us of God's goodness. He takes care of what belongs to Him, and we are His sheep. He takes us to green pastures and gives us protection and provision. He watches over us as a good shepherd, and when we follow Him, He leads us to places of peace.

In Prayer
God, thank You for Your goodness, protection, and provision to and for me. May I find rest in knowing You are my good shepherd.

Notes

_____

_____

_____

_____

_____

_____

_____

Day 16

Maker of the Heavens
. . . and Me

Pacific coastline at sunset, Olympic National Park, Washington

In the Word

"You alone are the Lord. You made the heavens, even the highest heavens, and all their starry host, the earth and all that is on it, the seas and all that is in them. You give life to everything, and the multitudes of heaven worship you." (Nehemiah 9:6 NIV)

In Context

In the book of Nehemiah, Nehemiah leads the Jews in rebuilding the wall around the city of Jerusalem. Babylonian King Nebuchadnezzar destroyed the walls 140 years earlier. After the Jews completed the rebuild, they had the priest Ezra read from the books of the Law, while the other priests who were with Ezra helped explain the law.

Most of the people had never read directly from the Law. When they finally heard it, they responded with great repentance and praise before God. For the first time in their lives, many of them understood His holiness and greatness. In celebration, the priests prayed the prayer in Nehemiah 9.

In Nature

Today, we know how vast the heavens are. Scientists say the universe contains hundreds of billions of galaxies. That number is far more than our human minds can truly comprehend.

The Hebrew priests did not have modern science telling them how vast the universe was, yet they knew it was great. They observed what you and I observe today when we behold the nighttime sky away from city lights. We don't need a scientist to tell us the heavens are great. We just need to open our eyes.

In Us

The Bible says God created and rules over the vast heavens. That's amazing! That same God cares for you and me. He not only names each star (Psalm 147:4), but He also numbers every hair on our heads (Luke 12:7). How wonderful to know that same great God who created the stars works in our lives today! Praise Him!

In Prayer

Dear Lord, like the ancient Hebrew priests, I praise you for being the maker of the heavens and the earth. You and You only are great!

Notes

_____

_____

_____

_____

_____

_____

_____

_____

Day 17

Not an Unknown God but an Unmade One

Pinnacles rock formation, Black Hills, South Dakota

In the Word

"The God who made the world and all things in it, since He is Lord of heaven and earth, does not dwell in temples made with hands; nor is He served by human hands, as though He needed anything, since He Himself gives to all people life and breath and all things." (Acts 17:24–25)

In Context

In Acts 17, the people of Athens wanted to hear about the new God that the apostle Paul proclaimed. They worshipped many gods already. So why not one more? At least, that's what they were thinking.

Paul began his reasoning with them in a way they would understand. He used nature and an altar they had built to an "unknown God." He told them that the God Who was unknown to them created everything and lives outside of creation.

Paul explained that his God was too great to live in a temple and did not need any help from men to exist. The God Who Paul proclaimed was a sharp contrast to the finite gods of the Greeks, so they needed to hear Paul's message.

In Nature

When people see nature, they see the hand of God. In our heart of hearts, we cannot look at the majesty of nature and not see God's hand.

The Bible is only available to those who have it, but everyone can look at nature and know that somebody had to create it. But still, people deny the existence of a Creator based on their own presuppositions and/or moral desires. When people look at nature without any presuppositions, they will see it as God's creation.

In Us

When you consider the wonders of nature, think about how great God is. How amazing does He have to be to create all that is in creation? From the tiniest bug to the greatest star, God made them all.

In Prayer

Dear God, when I look at creation, may it show me how great You are. For You have created wonders both tiny and great. I praise You!

Notes

_____

_____

_____

_____

_____

_____

_____

_____

Day 18

Everything That
Has Breath

Howling grey wolf, Nebraska

In the Word

Let everything that has breath praise the LORD. (Psalm 150:6 NKJV)

In Context

The word *praise* and its plural form *praises* fill the Psalms. The *New American Standard Bible* uses the word *praise* 147 times and uses the word *praises* twenty-three times, for a total of 170 times. Do you think the book of Psalms is trying to tell us something about the importance of praising God?

I find it fitting and significant that a book filled with praise ends with the line, *Let everything that has breath praise the* LORD. Not just people but everything with breath. The Hebrew word for *breath* is *nĕshamah*. The Hebrew Scripture not only applies *nĕshamah* to people and God but to animals.

In Nature

If the Scripture calls God's creatures to praise Him, how do they do it? In the case of wolves, He gave them a beautiful voice. On two different occasions, I have heard them howl. The sound is beautiful. God didn't have to make it beautiful. But He did. When wolves sing, the beauty in their voices praise God.

Another way animals worship God is by their very existence. When I look at a butterfly dancing between flowers or a great bull elk roaming the Rocky Mountains, I stare in awe and marvel at God.

Big or small, beautiful or muscular, gentle or dangerous, God's creatures cause me to wonder about our creative God and I worship Him in awe. What do all these diverse and magical creatures tell us about God? They tell us He is amazing!

In Us

If God calls amoral animals and all His creation to worship Him, how much more does He call us, whom He created in His image, to worship Him? Worshipping God comes in many forms. Often when we think of worship, we think of singing praise songs to God. So if you sing, sing with beauty, like the wolf.

Singing praise songs represents one form of worship. We also worship God by serving others, giving, living a moral life, staying true to His Word, and telling others about Him.

In Prayer

Dear Lord, help me not only to worship You with songs of praise but with my entire life.

Notes

Day 19

Our Rock

East Temple Rock, Zion National Park, Utah

In the Word

The Lord is my rock and my fortress and my deliverer, my God, my rock, in whom I take refuge; my shield and the horn of my salvation, my stronghold. (Psalm 18:2)

In Context

The Bible calls God a rock over two dozen times. In the Psalms alone, King David called God a rock twelve times. A study of the life of David shows that the fact that he called God his rock is very significant.

David conquered many foes as a victorious warrior and king, but he still called God His rock. He lived a life filled with great courage, strength, and fortitude that even today's best soldiers would admire, yet he clung to God as his ultimate source. The warrior king David knew that relying on God was not a weakness but a source of great strength.

In Nature

No finite object on earth can completely explain something about our infinite God but it can help us understand God better. When the Bible calls God a rock, it is using a metaphor to tell us something about Him. The rocks David saw stood powerful, strong, and everlasting. If you visit Isreal today, those very rocks still stand. David knew that the many qualities of the desert rocks apply to God, but only with God are those qualities infinite. The rocks will be gone someday, but God is truly everlasting.

In Us

What does it mean for God to be our rock? It means God is our stability in times of trouble. God always remains solid and unchanging. Though the world shakes and crumbles around us, God does not wobble. He stands solid and strong. In Him, we find salvation, not only from our sin but from the everyday troubles of this world. When the world makes us feel stressed, we can pick up a Bible and spend time reading its unchanging truths about God and what He gives us.

In Prayer

Dear God, I know You are my unchanging rock. Help me to rely on Your power, strength, and stability in times of trouble and every day. Thank You.

Notes

_____

_____

_____

_____

_____

_____

_____

Day 20

Stewards of What Belongs to God

Jenny Lake and Mount Teewinot, Grand Teton National Park, Wyoming

In the Word

The earth is the Lord's, and all it contains, the world, and those who dwell in it. For He has founded it upon the seas and established it upon the rivers. (Psalm 24:1–2)

In Context

Psalm 24 emphasizes God as King or that the Lord reigns. Verses 7–10 ask the question, *Who is this King of Glory?* Three times the psalm gives us the answer: "The Lord."

As Lord, God created everything, and it all belongs to Him. Every creature of the sea, every peak in the mountains, every planet in the solar system, and every star in the universe belongs to God. He created them all and owns them all, but as Genesis 1 and Psalm 8:6 tell us, God made us stewards over His creation.

In Nature

The next time you take a walk in nature, think about what you see. All of nature belongs to God—from the smallest wonder to the greatest ocean, even all the stars we see on the clearest night and those beyond them.

In Us

How does a good business manager handle a business that has been entrusted to him by the business owner? He treats it like it was his own business, right? Good stewards treat what belongs to someone else with care and respect—the way it was intended to be used.

God put us in charge of what belongs to Him. He has given us His creation for various reasons (food, labor, companionship, shelter, warmth, and power, etc.). We should use but not abuse what He has given.

In Prayer

Lord, help me to treat Your creation as something that belongs to You. Thank You for letting me experience it and use it but help me to always remember it is Yours.

Notes

Day 21

Highest Heaven

Pre-dawn sky over Turquoise Lake, San Isabel National Forest, Colorado

In the Word

"But will God indeed dwell on the earth? Behold, heaven and the highest heaven cannot contain You, how much less this house which I have built!" (1 Kings 8:27)

In Context

In 1 Kings 7, King Solomon, son of King David, completed the building of God's temple in Jerusalem. In chapter 8, the priests brought the ark of the covenant into the temple for the temple dedication. The presence of God dwelled in the ark and the priests placed the ark in the Holy of Holies. At that point, God's presence dwelt in the holy of holies. With humility, in 8:27, Solomon realized that God could not fully dwell inside the ark of the covenant, the temple, or any other building built by humans. God transcends all things in creation and is far greater than anything in the universe.

In Nature

When we ponder the depths of a clear blue sky, we feel really small. Or better yet, when we stand outside at night, far from the lights of a city and look at all the stars, we can really feel insignificant. But neither that vast clear blue sky nor the starry heavens can hold God. He transcends everything, meaning He exists outside of everything else. His transcendence is known as an incommunicable attribute of God, meaning only God possesses that quality. Only God is completely transcendent.

In Us

The heavens and the highest heaven transcend us, in that we cannot reach them, but the heavens cannot contain God. He transcends them. Yet this uncontainable God reaches down to you and me in space and time and dwells within us. We no longer need an ark of the covenant or a temple for the presence of God to dwell on Earth. He now dwells in the hearts of those who believe in Christ. Amazingly, the God that transcends the heavens has also chosen to dwell in you and me. Amen.

In Prayer

Dear God, let me feel Your presence in the everyday and may I glorify You for Your transcendence each day.

Notes

_____

_____

_____

_____

_____

_____

_____

Day 22

Glorious Splendor

Fall colors, Great Smoky Mountains National Park, Tennessee

In the Word

On the glorious splendor of Your majesty and on Your wonderful works, I will meditate. Men shall speak of the power of Your awesome acts, and I will tell of Your greatness. (Psalm 145:5–6)

In Context

Psalm 145 praises God for His greatness and for His works. It creates a beautiful picture of the majesty and glory of God as it mentions many of His divine qualities. The psalm uses forms of the words *great* four times and *praise* four times. It uses additional words like *awesome, abundant goodness, mighty, unsearchable, everlasting, gracious,* and *merciful* to describe God and His works.

Psalm 145 presents a clear message to the reader: God is great and beyond our understanding.

In Nature

Creation reveals so much of the glory and splendor of God. Think of how trees reveal God's glory and splendor and how they are one of His awesome acts. After the winter, they spring forth with delicate new leaves and bright blossoms. In the summer, they stand tall and green, soaking up the rays of the sun, harvesting its life-giving energy. In the fall, their hidden colors shine forth to touch our hearts with magic.

Trees and all creation present a clear message to the world: God is great and beyond our understanding.

In Us

The passage tells us to meditate on His wonderful works and that men will speak of His awesome acts. Think of all the different things God has created. What do they tell you about God? Think about everything God has given you and has done for you. What do those things tell you about God?

Some of His awesome acts happen around us, while others happen to us and in us.

In Prayer

Dear Lord, creation reveals so much of Your glory and splendor to us. If Earth holds all this beauty, how much more beauty awaits in Your eternal and perfect Kingdom?

Notes

_____

_____

_____

_____

_____

_____

_____

Day 23

Mount Up with Wings Like Eagles

Bald eagle taking off, Loess Bluffs National Wildlife Refuge, Missouri

In the Word
Yet those who wait for the Lord will gain new strength; they will mount up with wings like eagles, they will run and not get tired, they will walk and not become weary. (Isaiah 40:31)

In Context
In Isaiah 1–39, God condemned the nation of Judea for idolatry and a plethora of other sins. They turned their backs on the Lord and He pronounced judgment on them. The last thing Isaiah told Hezekiah in chapter 39 is that Babylon would destroy his kingdom during the reign of his great-grandsons.

In Isaiah 40–55, things changed. God prophesied to a future generation in exile. He spoke to them to restore their hope and to let them know that He would free them. He told them that they were not in exile because some fake foreign god defeated them but that their captivity was due to His discipline. By His power and authority, He promised He would rescue them and bring them home. In 40:31, He reminded them of His never-ending strength and that He imparts strength to those who wait on Him.

In Nature
Have you ever admired an eagle in flight? It is the picture of majesty, and it provides great inspiration. It's no wonder God inspired the prophet Isaiah to use eagles to encourage an exiled people. Eagles soar with ease and look like royalty doing so.

In Us
We may never find ourselves exiled in a foreign land, but we all experience tough times. In those times, think of a soaring eagle

and let it remind you of how God can lift you up. Call on God, and with His energy, mount up with wings like an eagle.

In Prayer

Dear God, thank You for eagles. Thank You for the picture they offer of Your energy beneath my wings, helping me to soar.

Notes

_____

_____

_____

_____

_____

_____

_____

Day 24

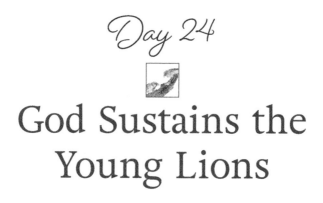

God Sustains the Young Lions

Male African lion

In the Word

The young lions roar after their prey and seek their food from God. When the sun rises they withdraw and lie down in their dens. (Psalm 104:21–22)

In Context

As an outdoor lover, I really like Psalm 104. The psalm praises God as not only the Creator of life but the Sustainer of life. It tells us how God remains active in His creation today by caring for plants, animals, and people. Psalm 104 proclaims God as the master gardener, the master zookeeper, and the Shepherd of His people.

In this psalm, we see that God provides not only for herbivores but also for the carnivores, like the young lions. Verse 21 says the lions, *seek their food from God.* And God gives it to them.

In Nature

Animals eating other animals was not God's original plan. In the garden of Eden, no animal killed another animal, but as a result of human sin, God's judgment fell on all creation. But praise God! One day, the Lord will restore creation to its original glory (Romans 8:18–22) and no animal will kill another ever again (Isaiah 65:25). Amen!

In Us

In this world, we experience hard times. Sometimes we even experience hard times from worldly persecution due to our faith in God. Throughout it all, God stays with us and provides for us, just as He provides for the lions. But like all creation, we, too, can look forward to that day when all creation be set free and *delivered from the bondage of corruption* (Romans 8:21 NKJV). Praise God and amen!

In Prayer

Dear God, thank You for Your daily provision for me and all Your creation. Give me the strength to live my life here. And give me the joy of knowing that one day, I will be free, living with You.

Notes

Day 25

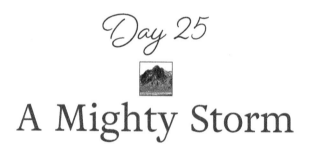

A Mighty Storm

Snow covered trees, Fontenelle Forest, Nebraska

In the Word

"He says to the snow, 'Fall on the earth,' and to the rain shower, 'Be a mighty downpour.'" (Job 37:6 NIV)

In Context

In Job chapters 3 through 31, Job and his three friends discussed the cause of Job's suffering. His friends tell Job it's because he sinned and God was punishing him. Job claimed he was a righteous man and his suffering was unjust. He complained to God and asked, *Why am I suffering?* He wanted an explanation from God, but he never received one.

In Job 32, a young man named Elihu entered the discussion to speak truth. He spoke about God's greatness, righteousness, and wisdom. He went on to talk about God's power over the weather to bring his point home (Job 36:32, Job 37).

In Nature

In the twenty-first century, humans still cannot control the weather. Every day in February 2019, at least one winter storm moved across the U.S. And record snowfalls fell throughout the upper Midwest. Then in March, the rains came. Combined with the melting snow, they brought extensive flooding. At least forty rivers crested at their highest levels ever recorded. In Nebraska alone, the flooding affected over 7,000 homes with damage estimated at $2.7 billion. Yet, with God, even the most powerful storms remain in His control. When He says cease, they cease.

In Us

God also holds power over the storms in our life. And just like the water from a rainstorm brings life and goodness, God uses the storms in our life to bring goodness. Though it may be difficult for us to see God's good purposes in the storms of life, we are called to trust Him through them.

In Prayer

Dear God, help me to see that You are working in and through me during the storms of life. Help me to trust You and grow in my faith when everything seems to be going wrong.

Notes

_____

_____

_____

_____

_____

_____

_____

Day 26

Trees of the Forest

Pine trees, Olympic National Park, Washington

In the Word

Then the trees of the forest will sing for joy before the LORD; *for He is coming to judge the earth.* (1 Chronicles 16:33)

In Context

This verse is part of a song that Israel's King David sang when the ark of the covenant was brought to Jerusalem. In it, David mentioned that the beauty of the forest sings to our God.

The second part of the verse mentions that God is coming to judge the earth. This references the coming of the Messiah to judge and redeem. All of creation rejoices at the work of Christ. All of creation will someday be redeemed.

In Nature

As my family and I hiked the trails of Indian Cave State Park in Nebraska, the trees seem to rejoice with a joyful autumn symphony. We love to hike in the fall, and the forest on this day seemed extra amazing. The colors of the singing trees created a serene peace in the warm glow of the sun. The trees led our hearts in praise. We could not help but sing with them.

In Us

Have you ever thought about how the trees praise God? They do so in the spring when their new leaves come forth and celebrate life and warmth. They do so in the summer when their leaves harvest the light of the sun, giving them the energy to grow strong. They do so in the fall when they display their glorious, hidden colors, pointing to their Creator. And finally, they do so in the winter when they silently stand as sleeping giants, giving refuge to the creatures who still need them.

The trees praise God in the everyday and so can we. When we are focused on loving God and loving others, we praise God and point others to Him.

In Prayer

Lord, help me to praise You and point to You in all I do, like the trees do.

Notes

Day 27

Away to the Wilderness

Rock formations in Badlands National Park, South Dakota

In the Word

But Jesus Himself would often slip away to the wilderness and pray. (Luke 5:16)

In Context

The Gospels mention about a dozen times that Jesus went to the wilderness to seek solitude. Luke 5:16 said He did it *often*. He did so in this particular passage to escape the crowds. In Matthew 4, Mark 1, and Luke 4, He did so in preparation to be tempted by Satan. Matthew also says Jesus tried to flee to the wilderness after learning of His cousin's death.

In Nature

The Scripture reveals that Jesus sought the presence, wisdom, and strength of His Father in the wilderness. Do you think Jesus may have known something about the importance of finding solitude in creation? Today, scientific studies tell us what Jesus knew— that nature is good for us. Science says the outdoors helps us clear our minds and empty our stress. And for the believer, it helps us hear from God and better connect with Him. God speaks to us through His creation, and the creation speaks to us about God.

On Earth, there is no better peace than the peace we find in the quiet of creation.

In Us

Jesus sets an example as He shows us the importance of getting outside. We should do it *often*, as He did.

In the outdoors, we provide ourselves with a great opportunity to hear from God. And it doesn't have to be the mountains or the ocean. We can find some quiet nature time in a park, local nature area, or in our own backyards. For some of us, it may be as simple as watching birds at a bird feeder. Get away to nature and God will speak to you.

In Prayer
Lord Jesus, You showed us that it's important to get away to the quietness of nature. Help me to make time to seek You in nature.

Notes

_____

_____

_____

_____

_____

_____

_____

_____

Day 28

"Call to Me"

Mountain valley, San Isabel National Forest, Colorado

In the Word

*"Thus says the L*ORD *who made the earth, the L*ORD *who formed it to establish it, the L*ORD *is His name, 'Call to Me and I will answer you, and I will tell you great and mighty things, which you do not know.'"* (Jeremiah 33:2–3)

In Context

In the days of Jeremiah, the Babylonians destroyed the city of Jerusalem and the entire Hebrew nation. God brought about the destruction due to the sins of the people. But in the midst of this calamity, God invited His people to *Call to Me.* Through Jeremiah, He said He would answer them and tell them *great and mighty things* they *did not know.* God promised them that the destruction would not last forever. He let them know in their deepest and darkest hour that He did not leave them.

In Nature

Once again, God used creation to show His people how great and powerful He is. He reminded them that He is the Creator, and although King Nebuchadnezzar and Babylon possessed great strength, their strength didn't compare to His. After all, He made the whole of creation.

The mountains, valleys, oceans, and wooded forests show us how great God is. He made them all and they are nothing but His footstool (Isaiah 66:1). If God made all of nature, then the greatest armies on the planet are nothing to Him.

In Us

God still says to us today, *Call to Me and I will answer you, and I will tell you great and mighty things, which you do not know.* When we despair, we can call to God. He wants us to call Him, even in our deepest, darkest hour. Call to Him in your hour of need and every day.

In Prayer

Thank You, God, that You want me to call to You. Thank You that You hear me and that You are always there for me. Amen and Praise You.

Notes

Day 29

God Holds the
Storehouses of Snow

Snow-covered road, Sarpy County, Nebraska

In the Word
"Have you entered the storehouses of the snow?" (Job 38:22a NIV)

In Context
Along with Psalms, Proverbs, Ecclesiastes, and the Song of Solomon, Job is one of the Bible's five books of poetry. With its poetic language, this book uses the word *snow* more than any other book in the Bible. In this verse, *snow* poetically tells us about God, that He is powerful.

In Job 38–41, God rebuked Job for his complaints. In these chapters, God used snow and other illustrations from nature to show Job that He is the creator, controller, and mastermind behind the wonders of nature. If Job had no idea how God controlled the world, then on what basis could he question God's judgment?

In Nature
Essentially, God said to Job, "I control the snow that covers the earth." Think about it. How amazing is that? God controls snow. The most powerful blizzard is nothing more than a breath to God. To this day, snow has the power to shut down life. Even in the most snow-ready cities, a heavy snowfall brings everything to a halt. Yet God holds the snow in His hands.

In Us
Life gets difficult and sometimes things happen to us that we cannot understand. In those times, we may question God. I know I do. And until this day, God personally answered few, if any of my questions. Instead, His answers to me are the same ones He gave to Job. What I need to do is take comfort in knowing that if

God controls the snow, then He is more than big enough to hold my life. The Lord knows what He is doing. And just like with Job, His purposes and plans lay outside my comprehension.

In Prayer

Dear God Almighty, You are the one who controls the snow. When life feels difficult or unfair, help me to trust You and all Your wisdom.

Notes

_____

_____

_____

_____

_____

_____

_____

_____

Day 30

Praise in Times of Stress

Sprague Lake, Rocky Mountain National Park, Colorado

In the Word

Be exalted above the heavens, O God; Let Your glory be above all the earth. (Psalm 57:5)

In Context

David wrote Psalm 57 while he was running from his enemy, King Saul. Saul's persecution of David put him under much stress, which you can detect in this psalm. In verse 4, he said his *soul is among lions.* In the midst of his time of tribulation, David cried out praises to God. Even when his heart was depressed, David recognized that God was to be praised.

We don't know why David wrote this particular line to praise God in the middle of his cries for help. Perhaps he was reaching out to God under a star-filled sky or at daybreak under a glorious sunrise, and while looking at the glories of creation, he remembered the greatness of His God.

In Nature

God shines His glory in the skies and in all of creation. I often feel the presence of God when I see the glory of creation. I am confident that David did too. He spent a lot more time in the wilderness than we do today. The words of many of his psalms reflect that the creation spoke to him about God.

Creation still speaks to us today about God. The skies all around the world are filled with His glory.

In Us

In our times of stress, it is good to go outside and look at the heavens. In the sky's greatness, we see God's greatness. When we realize how great God is in His creation, we have a better appreciation for His marvelous work in our lives. And we will praise Him like David.

In Prayer

Be exalted, O God, above the heavens; let your glory be over all the earth.

Notes

Day 31

Wherever We Go,
God Is There

Seagull over the Pacific Ocean, Southern California

In the Word

If I ascend to heaven, You are there; If I make my bed in Sheol, behold, You are there. If I take the wings of the dawn, if I dwell in the remotest part of the sea, even there Your hand will lead me, and Your right hand will lay hold of me. (Psalm 139:8–10)

In Context

This wonderful psalm declares how much God knows us. It tells us God knows so much about us that we cannot comprehend it (verse 6), and He understands all our thoughts (verses 2–3). Psalm 139 tells us we cannot escape from God's knowledge. His presence goes with us even to the ends of the earth (verse 9).

In Nature

When I stand on the beach, the ocean looks endless. I can only imagine how endless it must have seemed for ancient people. They had no idea what existed at *the remotest part of the sea* (verse 9). But David, the writer of Psalm 139, knew God would be there. He knew God would be with him wherever he went, just as God remains with each of us today.

In Us

I have read Psalm 139 so many times that the page has fallen out of my Bible. It's torn and tattered and I often have to place it back in my Bible. I have found refuge in this psalm, knowing that God stays with me, that He knows me perfectly, and that He believes in me despite my inabilities.

God has made us fearfully and wonderfully (verse 14), and He walks with us each day, no matter where we go. No matter what our physical shortcomings and/or lack of talents, God can and will use us.

In Prayer

God, thank You for knowing me and for being with me. Thanks for making me the way You have made me. Use me through Your knowledge of me and through the abilities You have given me.

Notes

_____

_____

_____

_____

_____

_____

_____

Day 32

Have All Heard?

Sunrise, Moraine Park, Rocky Mountain National Park, Colorado

In the Word

How then shall they call on Him in whom they have not believed?
And how shall they believe in Him of whom they have not heard
. . . But I say, have they not heard? Yes indeed: "Their sound
has gone out to all the earth, And their words to the ends of the
world." (Romans 10:14a, 18 NKJV)

In Context

In Romans 9–10, the apostle Paul discussed the mystery of the
Gentiles' salvation and the apostasy of the Jews. Paul wrote that
the message of God came through the Jews, but they rejected it
while the Gentiles received it.

He then asked the question, but how could anyone hear about
God if no one preached to them? He answered his own question
in verse 18 by quoting Psalm 19, saying there's always been a
preacher. God has continuously used His creation as His preacher.

In Nature

The History Channel has a television series called *Alone*. The
contestants on *Alone* have to make their own life in the wilderness with limited tools. They must find their own food and build
their own shelter as winter approaches. Often, they speak of how
they feel spiritually connected to the land, to the animals, and
even to the ancestors of the natives who lived there years ago.
They know there's something spiritual about nature, but they're
missing what that truly is.

I often sense something spiritual to nature, but nature itself
does not have a true, living "spirit." We sense something spiritual in nature because nature shouts out, "Someone made me!"

Nature displays the hand of God and speaks to the hearts of all people whether they recognize it correctly or not.

In Us

Nature speaks to every one of us, but we still needed to hear the gospel of Jesus Christ. Paul stresses the urgency that those who believe, need to proclaim the gospel. Nature does not take the place of the Christian foot soldier.

In Prayer

God, thank You for Your glorious creation that proclaims You. Help me to learn from Your creation that I, too, may proclaim Your glory and goodness.

Notes

Day 33

The God of Promises, Sunrises, Beauty, and the Inner You

Atlantic Ocean at sunrise, Melbourne Beach, Florida

In the Word

Thus says the Lord, who gives the sun for light by day and the fixed order of the moon and the stars for light by night, who stirs up the sea so that its waves roar; the Lord of hosts is His name. (Jeremiah 31:35)

In Context

In Jeremiah 31, God made several promises to the defeated nation of Judah. He promised the people of Judah that the Babylonians would not completely destroy them (verses 7, 10). In a second promise, God told them He would someday bring them back to Judah (verses 23–30). Finally, He promised to establish a new covenant with His people (verses 31–35). In case the people wondered how would God do this, He gave them a credibility statement in verse 33: *I will be their God, and they shall be My people.* He reminded the people that He made the sun, stars, and moon, and He gave the heavenly bodies their purpose.

In Nature

God created the sun. And to give you some idea about how big the sun is, according to NASA, "The Sun's volume would need 1.3 million Earths to fill it." That means the sun is huge! We cannot truly grasp the size of the sun God created.

The sun gives life and heat. That's all God needed to do with the sun to make it useful. But He did something else. He made sunsets and sunrises beautiful. With the sun, He provided not only for our practical needs but also for our need to see beauty.

In Us

Do you enjoy sunrises and sunsets? Our God is so great and so loves us that He gave us them to enrich our lives. He cares for our whole person: mind, body, heart, and soul.

In Prayer

Dear God, I praise and thank You for the beautiful things of life. Not only do I need the physical, but I also need the aesthetic things of life. Thank You for the gift of beauty.

Notes

Day 34

All the Peoples Have Seen His Glory

Post sunset sky, Sarpy County, Nebraska

In the Word

The heavens declare His righteousness, and all the peoples have seen His glory. (Psalm 97:6)

In Context

Psalm 97 shouts of the greatness of God. It declares that God is to be worshipped for His greatness, and the worship of other gods or idols is foolish and wicked. God's people worship Him and Him alone. And the glory of the skies tells us that God to be is worshipped.

In Nature

A few years ago, I worked as a gas pump attendant for a large warehouse club. Since most people pumped their own gas, I really didn't do much except observe and make sure simple needs were met.

One winter evening, right after sunset, the clouds beamed a glorious red and magenta against a deep blue sky. It was a marvelous view of nature above a busy suburban intersection. I paused, took in the amazing display of glory, and worshipped God. I then began to wonder how many people who were driving by and hurrying to their destinations even noticed it. And of those who noticed it, how many decided to pause and truly take it in? As Psalm 97:6 says, by way of the sky, *all the peoples have seen His glory.* But sadly, how few decided to appreciate it and to let it capture their focus?

In Us

God reveals His glory to us in nature. When we see it, we need to pause and take it in. It's a gift from Him.

God also reveals His glory to us through His word and by the way He works in and through people. When we read the Bible and pause to wonder about what we read, we get a greater appreciation for God's glory. And we also get a greater appreciation for His glory when we see Him work in people.

In Prayer
God, help me to praise You when You reveal Your glory through nature, the Bible, or through others. Amen.

Notes

Day 35

Eyes to the Mountains

Mountains, Great Smoky Mountains National Park, Tennessee

In the Word

I will lift up my eyes to the mountains; From where shall my help come? My help comes from the Lord, Who made heaven and earth. (Psalm 121:1–2)

In Context

Psalm 121 is one of the fifteen Psalms of Ascent. The Hebrew people sang the Psalms of Ascent as they approached Jerusalem on pilgrimages. They sang this particular song as they walked up from the valley floor below. It's believed that they sang this psalm antiphonal, which means a leader would sing one line and the people would respond with another. Knowing these two nuggets gives greater context to the words. The people looked up as they sang these four lines back and forth.

In Nature

My family and I live in the relatively flat state of Nebraska, but we love the mountains. Both my wife and I find mountains inspiring. Their size, height, and great strength bring out thoughts of transcendence. They remind us of our God.

Like mountains, God stands great and powerful, and He transcends all. When we cry to Him, our transcendent God hears us and comes to our aid. He is great and all powerful, able to meet our every need. If we think of a mountain as being mighty, how much mightier is our God Who created all the mountains?

In Us

Our help comes from the Lord. He is greater than anything in heaven or earth.

Sometimes, we find ourselves in situations that feel hopeless, but God is greater than any of our situations. And even though our problems will not always end the way we hope, we can trust that God is still in control. As the book of Job teaches, God has purposes beyond our understanding. We are called to rest in that and know that someday, we will spend eternity with Him.

In Prayer

God, help me to look to You at all times. My help comes from You. Mountains are great but they point to You as being greater. May they remind me of Your greatness.

Notes

Day 36

Summer and Winter

Snow-covered cornfield, Sarpy County, Nebraska

In the Word

"While the earth remains, seedtime and harvest, and cold and heat, and summer and winter, and day and night shall not cease." (Genesis 8:22)

In Context

This verse is part of the covenant God made with Noah and with all creation after the flood. Yes, there will be winter to rest the land, but there will always be spring to bring new life. After the spring, summer will come to grow the life, followed by fall to harvest God's bounty.

In His faithfulness to His creation, God will continue to bring the seasons. By the seasons, all creation receives provision from God.

In Nature

Nature is never stagnant. Each season brings something different and wonderful. Each season serves a different purpose. Summer allows time for growth and storing up energy; fall brings bounty and relief from the heat and bugs of summer; winter is a time for rest for creation and people; and spring brings new life, renewed hope, and new warmth.

Even in places with just two basic seasons, dry and wet, each season serves a unique purpose to aid the land and those who live on it.

In Us

God forever remains faithful to us. Just like the seasons come and go by God's purposes, seasons come and go in our lives under the authority of God's purposes. He faithfully remains with creation through the seasons and faithfully remains with us through our seasons of life.

God doesn't abandon creation in the winter. He designed that season. If God doesn't abandon His creation, we can be confident He will never abandon us.

In Prayer

Dear Lord, help me to see that the cycle of the seasons shows me Your faithfulness. Help me to also see that even the winter has its purpose and that You will remain with me and provide for me in the winters of my life.

Notes

Day 37

God Created the Sea
and All the Universe

Strait of Juan De Fuca before sunrise, Olympic National Park, Washington

In the Word

"Or who enclosed the sea with doors when, bursting forth, it went out from the womb; when I made a cloud its garment and thick darkness its swaddling band, and I placed boundaries on it and set a bolt and doors." (Job 38:8–10)

In Context

In Job 38, God used the foundations of creation to show Job how great and mighty He is. God essentially asked Job, "Did you make these things? Do you understand what makes them tick?" Job had no answer. In humility, he just sat and listened, then repented.

In Nature

My ten-year-old son loves watching the online program *Smarter Every Day*. The host (a father of young children) does all sorts of experiments to test different theories. The experiments show that scientific study can help us learn, but the experiments also show there is much that science doesn't know.

Like the show, scientists study and use the laws of physics. What scientists don't know is why the laws are what they are and who wrote them. Science leaves many questions unanswered. The Bible alone has the answer. Colossians 1:17 says that Jesus *is before all things, and in Him all things hold together.*

In Us

Like Job, most of us, and probably all of us (if we are honest), question God from time to time. I know I do, and I do it far too often. But who am I and who are we to question the infinite mind of God? The Bible tells us He created all things in this amazing world and universe. Can we really question the mind that designed the laws of physics, all the trillions of stars in the universe, and the beautiful wildflowers in a mountain meadow? Life works out best when we live in humility before our awesome God.

In Prayer

God, help me to live in wonder and awe of Your greatness. Keep me humble before You. You are truly amazing. Praise You!

Notes

Day 38

With Joyful Gratitude

Fall trees and sumac, Indian Cave State Park, Nebraska

In the Word

Shout joyfully to the Lord, all the earth. Serve the Lord with gladness; come before Him with joyful singing. (Psalm 100:1–2)

In Context

All nations and creation are called to praise God. And that praise is not supposed to be quiet. Verse 1 charges all the earth to *shout.* God is to be praised publicly and with great volume. Like the explosive beauty of creation, people are to sing to God in a way that makes a powerful statement about Him.

Psalm 100 also uses the words *thanksgiving, gladness,* and *give thanks.* A truly thankful heart realizes all that God has done and has no choice but to respond with joy and praise.

Thankful hearts praise God. Amen.

In Nature

The beauty and majesty of the creation compel us to worship its Creator. How can we see all the glorious wonders on this earth and not feel gratitude for our God? There's so much to see here and to take wonder in. The green trees, the blue sky, the singing birds, and the sound of a breeze all give us reason to praise Him.

In Us

God summons us to worship Him with others. To worship Him in nature is great, but God also calls us to worship Him corporately with other believers.

In the same way that I feel joy in creation, I feel joy in worshiping with other believers. When we shout joyfully to the Lord with others, we experience something powerful and draw closer to God. Worship is even more powerful when we sing with hearts of gratitude. A grateful heart sings with overflowing joy.

In Prayer

Lord, help me to make it a point to praise You and to sing with others. And help me to see all Your wonders and all You have given me that I may sing with gratitude.

Notes

Day 39

Everlasting Rock

Middle Cathedral Lake, Wind River Wilderness, Wyoming

In the Word
"Trust in the LORD forever, for in GOD the LORD, we have an everlasting Rock." (Isaiah 26:4)

In Context
Isaiah 26:1 sets the time period of this song of salvation for the chapter. *That day* in verse 1 is the day that God is victorious. Scholars say this could mean when Christ returns or at the end of the age or both. But whatever the specific day, *in that day*, we will find God to be our everlasting Rock. In Him, as our everlasting Rock, we will trust that our eternal salvation and peace are secure.

In Nature
On Earth, nothing lasts forever. Some things, like mighty rocks, give the illusion that they are secure and everlasting, but they will crumble someday.

When used as a metaphor, rocks give us a picture or an idea of the qualities of something that is everlasting. Something that is everlasting is strong, secure, stable, and unyielding. In heaven, we will trust with absolute confidence that God is our strength, security, and stability. Only God does not crumble or fade away. He is truly everlasting. He stands forever, stable and strong. He is the One our salvation will forever rest upon. He is our everlasting Rock.

In Us
Let's face it, even the most confident people have doubts and can be wishy-washy. Often, most of us experience doubt about our

abilities, life choices, and how others perceive us. From time to time, we may even doubt our faith. But after Jesus returns and brings us to live with Him, we will never doubt again. We will fully and forever trust God as our everlasting Rock. In Him, we will be secure.

In Prayer

Lord, help me to not doubt but to trust in You. Help me to know I can stand securely on You. May I know in my heart and mind that You are my everlasting Rock!

Notes

Day 40

Are We Special?

Hiker descending Mount Harvard, Colorado

In the Word

When I consider Your heavens, the work of Your fingers, the moon and the stars, which You have ordained; What is man that You take thought of him, and the son of man that You care for him? Yet You have made him a little lower than God, and You crown him with glory and majesty! (Psalm 8:35)

In Context

Psalm 8 begins and ends by declaring the greatness of God. The psalmist writes about God's glory and all that He has made. He then asked the rhetorical question, that in light of all creation, surely is not humankind insignificant? But instead of considering people insignificant, God made people in a way that resembles Him and the angels. With that distinction, He gave us a special place of honor above all other created things.

In Nature

Why do I photograph nature? Because I find it amazing and beautiful. Often, I desire to shoot something I've photographed dozens of times in the past. The wonders of God's creation continue to draw my affections. They never get old.

God made an amazing world, yet He made you more special than all other things in creation.

In Us

God has placed every person higher than the rest of His creation. No beautiful flower, nor majestic mountain, nor endless galaxy is more important to God than you. God loves you, has crowned you with glory, and has a purpose for you now and forever. No person is insignificant to God.

Take joy in knowing that God loves you and made you more significant than anything else in His vast and beautiful creation.

In Prayer

God, help me to see my significance in You and to You. May knowing how much You love me and value me give me a sense of purpose. Help me to know and see just how special I am in Your eyes.

Notes

_____

_____

_____

_____

_____

_____

_____

About the Author

P asquale Mingarelli has enjoyed God, photography, and the outdoors since his childhood. He graduated from Bowling Green State University in Ohio with a degree in photojournalism. After graduation, he worked with a newspaper in northwest Ohio. Following his time with the newspaper, Pasquale began working for *Worldwide Challenge*, an international Christian magazine published by Campus Crusade for Christ (now known as Cru). After twelve years with *Worldwide Challenge*, he left the magazine to celebrate God as Creator through photography.

In addition to *Worldwide Challenge*, his work also appeared in dozens of other publications including USAtoday.com, *Nebraskaland*, *Wildlife Conservation*, *Delta's Sky* magazine, the Billy Graham Evangelistic Association's *Decision* magazine, and school textbooks.

Currently, Pasquale helps photographers and others draw near to God through nature photography and he runs the website https://visualverse.thecreationspeaks.com. He also continues to work as a freelance photographer and lives in Bellevue, Nebraska, with his wife and two children.

Pasquale speaks on drawing near to God in creation. He is available to speak at your church, retreat, photography club, men's group, camp, or ministry event. You can contact Him through his website https://visualverse.thecreationspeaks.com or by email at pat@thecreationspeaks.com.

A free ebook edition is available with the purchase of this book.

To claim your free ebook edition:

1. Visit MorganJamesBOGO.com
2. Sign your name CLEARLY in the space
3. Complete the form and submit a photo of the entire copyright page
4. You or your friend can download the ebook to your preferred device

Morgan James
BOGO™

A **FREE** ebook edition is available for you
or a friend with the purchase of this print book.

CLEARLY SIGN YOUR NAME ABOVE

Instructions to claim your free ebook edition:
1. Visit MorganJamesBOGO.com
2. Sign your name CLEARLY in the space above
3. Complete the form and submit a photo
   of this entire page
4. You or your friend can download the ebook
   to your preferred device

Print & Digital Together Forever.

Snap a photo   Free ebook   Read anywhere

CPSIA information can be obtained
at www.ICGtesting.com
Printed in the USA
JSHW040450060523
41321JS00005B/6